NO COMPLAINTS, NO LAWSUITS

The Eleven Guiding Principles

of Quality Risk Management

Hal Denton and Fiona Lally

NO COMPLAINTS, NO LAWSUITS

Editor: Laurie R. Denton

Cover Design: Will Denton

Artwork: Francesca Lally

For Nick and Charlie
and for Francesca, Jude, Liam and Josephine

CONTENTS

Acknowledgements

We gratefully acknowledge the role of Dr. Urs Rainer von Arx, whose innovative work on quality management was essential to the formation of our book.

NO COMPLAINTS, NO LAWSUITS

The Eleven Guiding Principles

of Quality Risk Management

Hal Denton and Fiona Lally

INTRODUCTION

Almost three decades ago, when we began advising not-for-profit and other mission-driven organizations, risk management was a novelty for many clients. Most focused on risks to assets and litigation risks and believed that was enough.

> *Definition: "Litigation Risk* is the possibility of encountering legal action as a result of the organization's actions or inactions."

Today, brand and perception risks are not only amazingly high profile, they're also among the top concerns of businesses of all sizes and kinds. These risks arise from people's expectations and can be just as significant as classic asset and litigation risks. We could see that the traditional methods of risk management needed to expand to meet them.

The purpose of risk management is to minimize the likelihood and impact of potential loss; a *risk* being *a chance of loss*, and a *loss* being *a negative outcome*. In this book we

> *The goal of Quality Risk Management is to reduce the chance of loss for your organization and minimize the impact when losses occur.*

focus on managing risk arising from the allegation of liability, or from the idea that you were responsible for a loss, whether actually or just in someone's perception.

Insurance and other traditional risk management methods don't handle brand and perception risks well. This is because traditional risk management focuses on concrete losses, like when a court rules that an organization must pay a judgment or a case settles for a dollar amount. But a negative story posted on social media can create a different kind of big loss for any organization, even if the story is not true. And that's a loss insurance can't fix.

How does this happen? Poor reviews and online complaints can reach so many people so quickly that it is hard to react with the speed and effectiveness needed to control damage that occurs online. Lawsuits move more slowly, and losses associated with them are more concrete.

Organizations must now pay as much attention to complaints and unhappy customers as they do to litigation risks, because the losses they can cause are severe.

A good reputation can vanish in a day. According to Warren Buffett, "it takes 20 years to build a reputation and five minutes to ruin it." It's partly the velocity of these risks that make them both critical and difficult to manage.

Today's world requires a new approach to evaluating and managing risk, one that addresses both tangible and intangible losses; one that helps prevent complaints and unhappy customers, not just lawsuits.

By combining concepts behind both quality management and risk management, we have developed a new approach that succeeds in this environment. We call it *Quality Risk Management*. When we use the term *quality*, we don't mean producing the best of everything. We mean *delivering at the level your customers expect, in both big and small ways.*

The good news is that when you deliver at the level your customers expect, you reduce the risk of complaints. Not only does this protect your reputation and help satisfy your clients; it also helps build your brand—while reducing the risk of litigation.

Individually, we have advised clients extensively on legal, insurance, and risk management issues. As we worked for many of these clients, combining our respective areas of expertise and our risk management tools, we realized this combined approach is necessary to fully address every organization's risks today.

Quality Risk Management is based on concepts that are simple because they derive from a unified perspective on risk, grounded in the importance of delivering expected services and products. It is far more effective at addressing the complex needs of not-for-profit and other mission-driven organizations than the basic risk questionnaires we relied on years ago.

Our system combines traditional risk management and quality management techniques, founded in our professional experience, to provide the framework and tools you need to protect your organization from the full range of today's liability risks. By liability, we mean risks where you might be held responsible for something.

In *No Complaints, No Lawsuits*, we have distilled this approach into eleven Guiding Principles. Using these principles, you can quickly grasp how risks around responsibility arise and then determine how to manage them before—and after—they manifest.

These are simple steps that you and your organization can take now to understand the risks and be prepared for them. That preparation can help prevent losses, including brand damage, and reduce the impact of losses, including those that can't be covered by an insurance policy.

This book is for management, staff, board members, and volunteers concerned about managing the full range of liability risks, not just insurable risks.

Principles, Not Rules

Our system is built on principles rather than rules, because principles allow everyone in your organization to get involved in the risk management effort. We provide a framework that permits every person in your organization to think like a risk manager.

The job of a Risk Manager is to work with companies to *identify and treat potential risks* that may hinder the reputation, safety, security and prosperity of their organizations.

Anyone who wants to manage risk in today's volatile, accelerated environment has to understand how losses emerge—even intangible, uninsurable losses. This book provides the tools to do just that.

> *Over and over again, we find the Guiding Principles are the single most useful tool we offer risk managers and others who want to understand risk and reduce liability in their organizations.*

When you grasp the Guiding Principles, you'll understand immediately what is needed to avoid claims, complaints and lawsuits in your organization. Are you ready to start?

1

What is Quality Risk Management?

Definition: "Risk management is a system for identifying, reducing, avoiding, and transferring the chance of harm or loss."

D o you use checklists to do your risk management? We always did.

Like all risk managers, we've used them to systematically identify and evaluate hazards and liabilities, such as slippery floors, or transportation risks, or the kinds of problems that can arise from using volunteers.

These checklists showed us how hazards and responsibilities could turn into a problem if not well managed, but that was just the obvious part. We came to realize there is another kind of risk checklists don't capture.

It is the risk of loss arising from the *perception* of fault. The risk of not living up to something the public expects of you or your organization and for which they could hold you publicly accountable, whether you were to blame or not. This risk, based on peoples' expectations, has become critically important to understand and manage, as social media continues to change the way we experience the world and operate our businesses.

Organizations often struggle to grasp how it is that something they feel is not a real risk—a complaint they believe is unfounded or a claim they feel is not reasonable—could cause so much damage.

This expectation risk has a huge potential impact because it can still produce complaints and lawsuits whether fault is there or not. In many ways it is the risk that needs management the most, because it can lead to losses that can't be insured: like the loss of reputation, morale, funders or volunteers.

We found this expectation risk tough to describe. Customers and other stakeholders, however, know it the minute they see it.

When there is an accident, an incident or a problem, we often hear people say:

> "They should have known about this."

> "They should have done something about this."

> "They should not have let this happen."

> "You've got to be kidding me."

> "I expected better."

> "They shouldn't be able to get away with this."

That "they" could be you. And this is how a complaint or a lawsuit is born.

In the modern era of social media, where complaints can spread like lightning and affect your organization overnight, it's critical that you manage people's expectations, whether they are realistic or not.

Most organizations pay close attention to the risk that someone could get injured while participating in their activities, for example, and doubtless you do, too.

What's not always clear is the way you could be held responsible when the injury occurs, even if you think you have handled everything right.

> *The biggest reason people complain and sue is because of what they expected was going to happen, not necessarily what actually happened.*

The real question is - what did people expect you should have done? How did they expect you to respond? Not knowing how the public might perceive your responsibility for the outcome makes it hard to fully manage the losses that could emerge. And, unfortunately, unrealistic expectations can damage your organization just as much as realistic ones.

Over time we figured out how to incorporate the perception part into our risk management approach. The key to finding out what people expect is to add quality management principles to traditional risk review in your overall risk management program.

Once you look at risk through the prism of people's expectations, you can much more fully understand the ways that a risk can turn into a loss, and what to do about it. That is what sets Quality Risk Management apart from all other approaches to risk management.

The eleven Guiding Principles break these kinds of expectations into components so you can systematically build their impact into your risk management system.

All the Guiding Principles are based on the idea that liability risk comes from an array of expectations that someone has about your organization—whether you know about or agree with their thinking.

Now you have a way of managing the range of liability risks that can affect your mission-based organization. These can range from traditional legal arguments around negligence, to a parent's angry complaint about a playground scrape, to a loss of funders after a negative experience that plays out in social media.

2

What Causes Complaints? What Causes Lawsuits?

Most lawsuits against not-for-profit and mission-driven organizations allege harm arising from negligence, presumably caused by something your organization did or didn't do. In this book, *your organization* means both your organizational entity and all the people helping deliver your products and services.

Traditional risk management focuses on potential loss of assets and legal challenges. It's all about making people whole from a loss they believe happened to them. When lawsuits come down to money, that's where insurance policies can help, because financial loss is what they insure.

Definition: "Insurance is a contract where one party agrees to accept certain kinds of risk from another in exchange for premium."

Unmet expectations and the complaints that accompany them can have the same damaging effect as tangible losses.

But money is only part of the issue when there's a lawsuit. What other losses or negative outcomes can we expect from a claim or legal challenge? A fine reputation can be lost. Funders and customers could vanish. And this can happen even if you win the lawsuit, and even if you were not at fault.

Morale can also be affected. Mission, programs and opportunities can be derailed. These losses are real, even if they're not tangible or quantifiable. Unfortunately, they are losses insurance can't cover.

Complaints and unmet expectations can harm your organization even if there is no demand for payment, and even if you think they're undeserved.

How is it that an organization might believe it did everything right and still get slammed by a story on the Internet? And in a connected world, how can your organization prevail when things really do go wrong?

Quality Risk Management views these losses—from the biggest lawsuits to the smallest annoyance claims—as arising from the same source: unmet expectations.

Dissatisfaction can play out in courtrooms or in social media. One way or another, people are seeking remedies to what they see as your organization's failure to meet a standard, fulfill a brand promise or meet their expectations.

Anatomy of an Expectation

It's not only a bad outcome, such as an injury or a faulty product that can deliver a loss. A perception that your organization did not perform as expected can create a loss too.

In our society people typically feel that someone should be held responsible for any bad result.

Let's say your organization experiences a computer problem, like a website crash. It results in customer confusion and a series of complaints. Such a snafu can cause a crisis that might be bigger than the computer problem itself. You may not have been responsible for the problem, but you take the heat for it.

The reverse is also true. Even after some terrible problems, it's possible for your organization to gain understanding and even respect from customers. It's possible to go on to thrive from positive public assessments about the way you have handled a problem or complaint.

Tylenol made a hero of Johnson & Johnson: The recall that started them all

By Judith Rehak
Published: March 23, 2002

It has been almost two decades since a consumer products company's worst nightmare became tragic reality for Johnson & Johnson. In the space of a few days starting Sept. 29, 1982, seven people died in the Chicago area after taking cyanide-laced capsules of Extra-Strength Tylenol, the painkiller that was the drugmaker's best-selling product.

Customers, government agencies and third parties are constantly judging your organization. Your responsibility is to know the basis of that assessment—to understand how your performance is being measured and how your organization might be held accountable.

Using Quality Risk Management, you'll find that it's not enough simply to conduct liability and hazard reviews to manage risk. From the start, organizations need to frame their risk analysis from the viewpoint of the expectations by

> *Ultimately, people measure your organization by their expectations. Those expectations could arise from a standard, a law, an internal policy, or even a misunderstanding about the nature of what your organization does.*

which they are being measured. That's an essential element of the eleven Guiding Principles.

Each Guiding Principle informs a different aspect of the risks your organization faces. Were you responsible for that computer problem, for example? Was a commenter justified when complaining that they didn't expect this to occur in working with you? Were the circumstances that led to the computer problem reasonably evident? Could the organization have taken reasonable steps to address them?

If the answer to any of those questions is *yes*, that informs the risk management tasks, and Quality Risk Management can guide you in how to proceed.

If the answer is *no,* then you still must take steps to address the expectations in play. You may not have been responsible for the computer issue, but you're still on the receiving end of a negative public reaction, often the most overlooked part of effective risk management. Quality Risk Management helps you with this, too.

Living Up to Expectations

Determining and living up to some expectations can be straightforward. People don't expect sugar in their salt shakers. But some people's expectations of your organization may be unachievable, unrealistic, or downright crazy. You can't be expected to turn sugar into salt!

But even if an expectation is unreasonable, it could lead to a complaint or even a lawsuit, and that can cause a loss. Fortunately, you can identify and manage unreasonable expectations very effectively using Quality Risk Management.

> *Managing expectations is not the same as assuming liability for everything that happens or trying to control every outcome. It's not about trying to be the best at everything.*

This approach to risk management allows your organization to prepare for and respond to the liability risks the Guiding Principles reveal. It helps promote realistic expectations about your organization.

The first step in determining what is realistic is to evaluate the legal principle of negligence and the role it plays in setting expectations.

Negligence

The primary liability concern for most organizations is negligence. When organizations are sued and have to pay damages, the claim is usually based on the laws of negligence.

> *Definition: "What is negligence?* **Let's keep it simple and define it as failing to act reasonably under all circumstances."**

Understanding negligence and managing the risks associated with it are a key element of Quality Risk Management and the Guiding Principles.

This description of negligence may seem clear, but we need to break it down a bit more to fully appreciate the depth and breadth of the responsibility it imposes.

The United States and, increasingly, other countries promote a safety-conscious environment with a low tolerance for outcomes that result in accident, injury or illness. The world is raising its expectations around safety. This can affect you even if you believe you acted reasonably.

Once you evaluate your organization's risks with the Guiding Principles in mind, you will be well equipped to understand the concept of negligence and the power of expectations, and how they affect your organization.

Think of someone getting seriously hurt on a school or municipal playground while using a piece of playground equipment. It's easy to imagine that occurrence turning into a lawsuit. But what is the actual legal basis for the lawsuit?

We will break out the critical legal concepts of negligence that underpin overall risk management.

You will then see how you can be held responsible for outcomes.

We tie these concepts to principles of managing expectations so you can address liability risks of all shapes and sizes.

This can help you manage risks ranging from a little complaint to a black swan event that results in a bell-ringing lawsuit.

> *Definition:* "A *black swan* is a rare event that is hard to predict and has a very significant impact."

In the chapters that follow, we'll explain each of the Guiding Principles and how they help you reduce the chance of loss. We'll give examples, along with the legal, risk and quality management fundamentals that apply to each.

We'll also provide key takeaways and implementation tips to apply Quality Risk Management in your organization.

3

The Guiding Principles

Let's get to the eleven Guiding Principles, what each one means, how they relate to each other, and, most important, how to use each one to build a good risk management program that addresses the range of risks and expectations that affect you and your organization.

For us, these principles are essential. Ignore them at your peril!

1. *You can't guarantee safety, but you must identify and manage risks.*

2. *You have a duty to disclose known risks.*

3. *Assumption of risk requires prior informed consent.*

4. *If you ask for information, you have to do something with it.*

5. *When you act, you have to act reasonably.*

6. *Treat people the same unless there's a good reason to treat them differently.*

7. *You can be held responsible for third parties if you have sufficient control over them.*

8. *Meeting expectations avoids claims; therefore, meeting expectations is a key element of managing risks.*

9. *Standards help manage expectations, but having a standard you don't follow is worse than not having one.*

10. *You have a duty to be aware of and to comply with standards that apply to your organization.*

11. *A compassionate response is a critical component of managing expectations—especially when the loss is significant.*

Guiding Principle 1.

You can't guarantee safety, but you must identify and manage risks.

> *We live in a world where many people believe that if something goes wrong, someone else is to blame and should pay for the loss.*

We live in a risky and hazardous world. Consider a hazard as something that presents a danger, and a risk as a chance that some kind of loss or negative outcome could result.

Every time we leave home, we risk injury, illness or loss. Even staying at home is no guarantee of safety.

Complaints about bad results take on new meaning in an era of social media, where reputational damage can happen in a matter of hours. How can we be expected to organize our activities and navigate this minefield? Some

organizations believe that if they aren't aware of a risk, they won't be held accountable for it. Some are bent on presenting what they do as safe to avoid scaring people off, while others regard taking on risk as a form of authenticity. The effect is to handle risk as if it were a totem, something mystical, to be feared and maybe not fully understood.

Often people consider good past results as a reason not to be concerned about what might happen in the future. It's a trap into which an organization can easily fall. Frequently people will tell us that things have been going well, and that they don't want to jinx anything by looking at their risks too closely.

Good risk management, however, has to be a continuous effort to identify, manage, and monitor risk. A hopeful reliance on past good fortune isn't enough. A "hear no evil, see no evil" view of the world is sure to leave you unprepared.

When identifying risk, focus your attention on two main issues:

> 1) keeping people safe, and

> 2) protecting the organization's ability to carry out its mission.

Explore the risks that could adversely affect these two main points. Often people focus on familiar smaller or mid-range risks and overlook the bigger ones. It helps to start by assessing the most significant risks to your organization, then narrowing down.

Succeeding at risk management requires organizations to take a thoughtful, measured approach. Not knowing that a risk exists, or pretending that it doesn't, does not absolve you from the responsibility for managing it. Your organization is expected to do a reasonable job of identifying and managing risks, while avoiding the false expectation that an activity or product is entirely risk-free.

How do you strike the right balance? Quality Risk Management provides the roadmap every manager, volunteer or employee can use to support your risk management efforts. Because it involves managing both risks and expectations, it helps keep people safe *and* reduces people's natural tendency to blame someone else for any bad result.

Identifying Risks

It's reasonable to take appropriate steps to manage identified risks. Because this expectation is broadly accepted, it can create liability if these steps are not taken.

> *There is a duty to identify known risks, because it would be negligent not to do so. It's what a reasonable person would expect under the circumstances.*

Imagine that you are the president of a small organization that operates rural bicycling tours, and one of your customers is severely injured. This first Guiding Principle asks you to consider whether the injury was foreseeable. If it was, and if you failed to consider this by, for example, not bringing a first aid kit or planning for a medical evacuation, your organization is placed in a difficult position.

Even if your actions were not negligent, it is far better for your organization to be able to list all the preparatory steps you took than to say, "I wish we had thought of that," "that never happened before," or "we were planning to hire someone to work on that."

No Guarantee of Safety

While any reasonable organization needs to identify risks associated with its activities, it isn't possible to identify every risk. Things go wrong every day that are hard to imagine ahead of time. It's those things that you *can* reasonably imagine that need attention. For the others, you need to manage expectations by not over-promising safety.

As you work through ways of managing the risks you have identified, it's often clear that some risks can't be eliminated. You may be able to reduce the likelihood they will occur or the severity of the impact if they do, but life is, at a very basic level, risky.

Even on a simple walk on a flat trail in the woods, you can't entirely eliminate the risk of tripping and falling, or of something unexpected occurring. That's why it is so important that organizations not sugarcoat the risks they foresee or over-promise safety.

An organization that arranges bus tours overseas, for example, needs to let its travelers know the degree to which safety requirements around cars and buses in their tour countries can differ from the travelers' experience at home. There is a great deal of excellent material available on the internet in areas like this. Look for reputable sources to inform the way your organization manages these risks.

> *People are aware that they face risks everywhere. Over-promising safety changes people's expectations about risk; that can lead to complaints.*

It is far better to turn your customers into risk managers with you by advising them of the range of risks and the ways they can stay safe, than to lead them to believe there are no risks or that you have managed them all. Downplaying risk can also create the basis for liability because people may justifiably rely on your commitments and then fail to take steps to protect themselves because they assumed your organization had everything covered.

Alert people to the range of risks they may encounter in connection with your activities. If you've done your reasonable best to keep them safe with appropriate risk management methods, let them know, but state frankly that this may not address everything that can happen. If someone is unwilling to participate under those terms, it is far better to know this early. Consider this part of effective screening.

As you consider each of the Guiding Principles, keep in mind that this duty requires that you balance being an effective risk manager with being an effective expectations manager. This is Quality Risk Management in action.

Consider the U.S. government slogan, "If you see something, say something," launched to help combat terrorism. This slogan appears throughout the New York City subway system. Those six words immediately convey that there are risks when riding the subway, and that every rider is being asked to stay alert and support safety in the subway.

Be the best risk manager you can be, but avoid minimizing the risks you find, or falling into the trap of guaranteeing that any activity is absolutely safe.

KEY TAKEAWAYS

- Organizations have an obligation to identify and manage risks associated with their operations.

- Quality Risk Management involves managing both risks and expectations.

- Once you identify risks, you have a duty to manage those risks.

- Rather than over-promise safety, make people aware of known risks so they can also help manage those risks.

Implementation Tip 1: Put together a group of risk analysts from your organization. If you can, bring in people from different areas, such as management and field activity. Offer donuts. Ask them to spend a morning homing in on *1) safety risks* and *2) risks so big they could shut down the organization or derail its mission.* Have someone write every risk down in the different ways it may emerge, even if it seems repetitive. Later, you'll be able to use that information to establish the major risk themes in your organization.

Guiding Principle 2.

You have a duty to disclose known risks.

Once you identify risks associated with your activities, you have a responsibility to take steps to manage those risks. Part of that duty includes the obligation to let others know the potential risks.

From signs like "Thin Ice" or "Beware of Dog," we understand this principle implicitly, yet when it comes to managing risk, sometimes organizations want to go easy on letting others truly understand the risks. They fear their customers will be scared away.

This is an unfortunate mistake, because downplaying or failing to reveal risk does not change your legal obligation under basic negligence law. It's reasonable to let people know when they are taking risks, in part because it enables them to take steps to protect themselves. Conversely, it isn't reasonable and it is risky to keep people in the dark about risks you know about.

> *Every organization has to balance the positive aspects of its programs, products, or services with adequate disclosure of the risks involved.*

It may seem tempting not to look into the risks associated with your organization's activities to avoid having to disclose known risks. Sometimes people tell us, wishfully, that ignorance *is* bliss, because knowledge brings so many responsibilities.

Unfortunately, this is not a viable option because, as we learned from the first Guiding Principle, organizations have a duty to identify and manage risks associated with their programs, activities, and products. And once you know about something that could be important to your stakeholders, you are expected to disclose it.

People often ask us if those macabre lists of possible bad outcomes are really necessary, such as recounting the sometimes-bizarre possible side effects in prescription drug commercials, or the copious risks people are told about before surgery. The answer is that if listeners might reasonably rely on that information in deciding to go forward, they need to hear the full range of risks. You might also ask yourself if you would like to have that information if you were in their position.

Protection from Disclosure

Assuming you have done the work required and have identified the risks, disclosing them to your customers and other stakeholders helps protect your organization and your customers in two ways.

First, it helps people decide whether they're prepared to assume the risks associated with the activity. Once advised, some people may choose not to participate. You should not view this as a negative. You may be screening out people who probably *should* avoid the activity, either because it isn't appropriate for them, or because they have unrealistic expectations about the risks involved.

The person who decides against what you have described as a strenuous hike might have a heart condition. Someone with a pre-existing condition like a bad knee could decide to avoid contact sports. It is helpful to avoid having people participate who would only end up complaining later, or filing a claim.

Second, risk disclosure can shift some of the responsibility for those risks from your organization to others. For example, the risk of a mosquito-borne illness can be mitigated by common sense protective measures. If you're organizing a trip in a location where there is a mosquito-borne illness risk, letting your participants know this in advance and advising them on the steps they can take to protect themselves helps to mitigate the risk. This turns your participants into risk managers themselves, which can prevent losses.

Disclosing such known risks serves several purposes:

- It reduces the likelihood of illness or injury.

- It reduces the likelihood of a complaint or claim because people can better evaluate whether the activity is right for them.

- It helps you meet your legal obligation to act reasonably under all circumstances.

KEY TAKEAWAYS

- Your organization has a duty to disclose known risks.

- Disclosing known risks transfers some of the responsibility to others

- Disclosing known risks helps avert negligence claims and reduces complaints.

- Making people aware of the risks involved helps them manage those risks and reduce the likelihood of injury or sickness.

Implementation Tip 2: When you tell people about risks involved with your organization in a description of your programs or services, for example, your mantra should be: what would people *reasonably expect to know.*

Guiding Principle 3.

Assumption of risk requires prior informed consent.

When you have identified a risk, a tried-and-true method of managing it is to transfer the risk to someone else. We touched on this in the second Guiding Principle about acting reasonably by disclosing known risks.

Insurance is a classic form of risk transfer, because the insurance company takes on your risk by contract (the insurance policy) in return for premium. Transfer is at the heart of the risk management method called *assumption of risk.*

> Definition: *"Assumption of Risk* is when someone knowingly recognizes the risks associated with an activity but decides to do it anyway."

Waivers, releases, permission slips, and acknowledgements all involve varying degrees of assumption of risk. The person signing the document gets to do something in return for agreeing to be responsible for some or all of the outcomes.

We're often asked if this kind of transfer strategy really works. The answer is yes. But it must be done properly to meet legal requirements and the expectations of the person using it. A badly framed assumption of risk document may not be enforceable and can create complaints.

Permission Slips are the simplest form of assumption of risk. They generally refer to something specific that warrants a risk transfer. An example is parental permission for a child to go on a field trip, perhaps because it's something unusual for the organization to do.

Acknowledgements are declarations by the signer of something being true, like receiving something, possibly as simple as having received certain information.

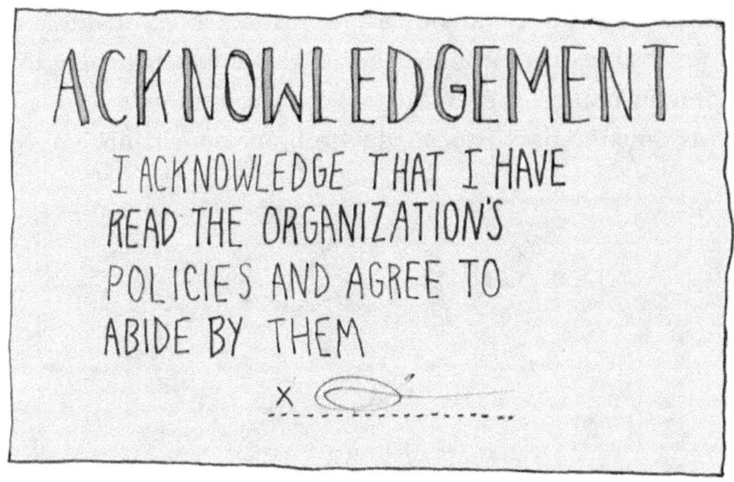

How Risk Transfer Documents Work

People often mistake how these documents work. They'll say, "Look! He can't sue me, he signed that form!"

Actually, anyone can lodge a lawsuit or present a claim at any time. The existence of assumption-of-risk documents doesn't stop people from suing or making claims, but it can help prevent people from being *successful* when suing or making claims.

These documents can also help reduce complaints and resolve disputes before going to court by reminding those involved about what had been agreed to previously. This can be an effective way of managing expectations.

Remember that the heart of this strategy is to transfer risk from one party to another. What makes that transfer successful?

Transfer of Risk, the underlying tenet of insurance transactions, is a risk management technique to shift risk from one party to another. Risks may transfer between individuals, from individuals to insurance companies, or from insurers to reinsurers. For example, when people buy home insurance, they are paying for an insurance company to assume the risks associated with home ownership.

Under U.S. law, a person can't really take on a risk and assume responsibility for the result of something unless she or he is fully aware in advance of the risk being assumed. This results in a lot of strenuous efforts to make people aware of risk, often with tons of off-putting information, sometimes described in tiny print and legal jargon.

Anyone who has gone whitewater rafting or skydiving has seen the extensive risk disclosures these kinds of service providers use, listing every possible frightening outcome. It can seem excessive, but this is because the range of serious outcomes is otherwise not typically known, or tends to be discounted. The idea is that unless you're fully aware of all the risks, you're not in a position to accept them.

Is signing a form or listening to an ad for medication on TV the same as getting informed consent? This is where typical risk management often fails, and the issue of managing expectations comes in.

Permission slips are common for special school activities. They typically come in two forms: a blanket form and a detailed form seeking informed consent.

Permission Slip

I GIVE PERMISSION FOR THE ORGANIZATION TO USE MY IMAGE FOR THE SPECIFIED PURPOSES

Generally, if the risks are not adequately disclosed and clearly accepted, then the risk transfer can't be successful. Put yourself in the position of parents signing a permission slip for a field trip. The question is: does the slip describe the entire trip fully enough to permit the parents to make an informed decision or raise an objection if the parents think it isn't appropriate for their child?

The expectation is that the permission slip provides sufficient information for readers to make an informed choice and possibly decide not to participate. "I knew you were going bungee jumping…. I just didn't know it was off of a cliff!" Meet that expectation and the permission slip can work on two levels, because meeting expectations helps avert complaints and lawsuits. This is a less legalistic approach that works well, especially when lengthy legal documents are not advisable or appropriate.

Remember, we are approaching risk management from the perspective of concepts and principles in this book, not rules. Counsel should review any legal documents, but understanding the principles involved allows you to be an effective risk manager at all times, even in unfamiliar situations when your organization may not have rules to guide you.

We know that acknowledgements are declarations that something has been read, signed, received or agreed to. But like any other attempt at risk transfer, if there is no informed consent, there is probably no risk transfer. Checking a box saying you have read and understood the terms of use of a website may suffice...but it may not.

> *General or blanket permission slips that don't differentiate one event from another aren't useful. They don't give enough detail to allow for informed consent.*

If the wording is commonly accepted, that may be enough. But it's not reasonable for a software maker or a website owner to expect that checking *yes* will lead to informed consent from the typical consumer if there are unfamiliar or unusual terms in a document.

Consumers expect to sail through these consent processes without special knowledge. They often find the language impenetrable in the consent documents anyway. Meanwhile, organizations don't want to be overly burdensome or call attention to things that may scare people away. Both parties have skewed expectations. Risk transfers set up in this manner need better management.

Some years back, there was a class-action suit against a social network for using its customers' images to sell products. The terms of use authorized the company to use these images, but the users of the social network did not foresee their use for commercial marketing. That case was settled with the company agreeing to make its terms of use more clear about 1) the use of customer images for commercial purposes and 2) the parental control features available to manage use of the images. This case illustrates the need to meet consumer expectations in a clear, upfront way, rather than trying to secure legal protection with small type or hard-to-find links on a website.

Waivers are the most technical of these risk-transfer methods. They are legal documents and must be framed by a lawyer to hold up in court. It's not a good idea to duplicate another organization's waiver without legal guidance.

With a waiver, the signer waives certain rights, such as the right to sue.

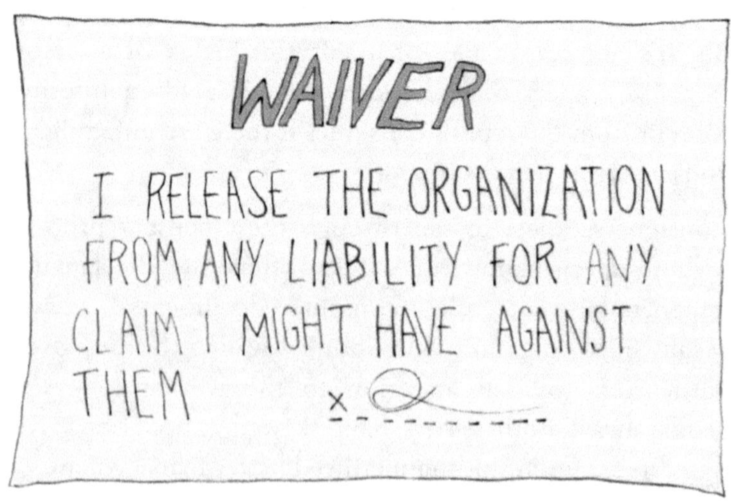

Some forms of negligence really can't be effectively transferred, no matter how strong the waiver document. Courts don't allow every kind of risk to be assumed by others. This is why it's often best to use a waiver as a deterrent to a lawsuit and to focus on removing or reducing liability by other means.

In general, for a court to allow people to waive their right to sue and transfer the risk and its outcome to the people waiving those rights, the information provided must meet an exceptionally high standard. When a waiver can effectively transfer risk, it's because it was able to offer fully informed consent.

KEY TAKEAWAYS

- Permission slips, acknowledgements, and waivers are all valuable risk management tools that can transfer risk from one party to another.

- Permission slips and acknowledgements help manage expectations by giving information to others who can use it to make informed decisions.

- Waiver documents require careful drafting because people are waiving legal rights. Waivers are generally effective only when there is fully informed consent.

Implementation Tip 3: Ask similar or peer organizations for examples of their risk transfer documents when creating your own. If you find examples of permission slips or acknowledgements that *fully inform*, you can use those as inspiration for yours. However, don't use a waiver—a document that gives up legal rights—if a lawyer hasn't specifically built it for your purposes, even if it looks compatible to you.

Guiding Principle 4.

***If you ask for information,
you must do something with it.***

We live in an age that's jam-packed with information streaming through the ether. Typically, we view information as an asset, and these days, something easily searchable. We might pursue a good range of detail on someone's personnel application to be really thorough in evaluating a candidate; we might accumulate a slew of background information to develop a great program.

But having all this information is not carefree or risk-free. Remember the Guiding Principle that says that you must manage risks once you become aware of them?

You're equally responsible for acting on information you have. One important risk management tool is: *be thoughtful about the information you request.*

When asking for information, organizations should consider four issues:

1) Why do we need this information?

2) What are we going to do with it?

3) How long will we keep it?

4) What tools do we have to ensure information is properly acted on, protected, and stored?

Sometimes the liability created by requesting information is inadvertent.

Organizations might ask for say, personal information for marketing that might create a liability in another area, like cyber security.

Sometimes the liability is direct. Don't ask for anything in a personnel application, for example, that you don't intend to use. Take out questions that are not directly relevant to your operations. This reduces the amount of data you must store and protect. Finally, make sure you have permission from the person whose information you're gathering to use that information in the way you intend.

Then, make sure you can account for every piece of personal information you get. If you asked for three references, for example, there is liability in not pursuing all three, even if the first reference sounds just fine and you need to hire quickly.

Bad circumstances don't generally provide you with cover when it comes to avoiding negligence in this area, which is closely related to the fifth Guiding Principle: *Once you act, you have a duty to act reasonably.* Imagine putting a child in a hosting placement when one of your references would have told you that he or she would never allow his or her own children in that family's home, but you failed to check.

Liability From Information

Not having the resources—personnel, expertise, or funding—to fully manage information may be a very real burden for your organization. But it doesn't relieve you of the responsibility that comes with having obtained data that must now be reviewed, acted on, and protected. It's not considered reasonable to gather information that can inform your operations and your risk management approach and then ignore it.

This is true even if a well-intentioned organization asks for information as part of a program for which it later loses support or funding. Let's say an organization starts to collect volunteer driving records as part of a new transportation safety program. Unfortunately, funding for the safety program is withdrawn after only a year, and away goes the only person who knows how to make sense of the drivers' records. The records remain compiled and unanalyzed, while volunteers continue to drive on behalf of the organization.

Consider what could happen if one of those drivers causes a crash and has a dismal driving record that could easily be located on a database at the organization. What would that mean for the organization? It's in hot water because it asked for and received information it reasonably should have used to keep that driver off the road while on organization business.

This kind of information can be a bombshell in a lawsuit. Once you have information, think about how you are expected to use it, and then about its legacy. Keeping information longer than you need it creates all sorts of additional risks.

Laws in most places now generally require you to obtain permission from people before gathering and processing their personally identifiable information. The third Guiding Principle on assumption of risk provides the insight to consider what to include in that permission. It should fully inform the people you are asking about the purpose, use, storage, and protection of the data requested, and their consent should be clear.

You must protect personal information for as long as you have it to meet privacy expectations. That's one reason to keep it no longer than necessary.

Keeping personally identifiable information longer than needed may also violate data protection laws. It can create further problems in future litigation, when you may be asked to provide the court and opposing counsel with vast amounts of information that could help the other side. The cost of producing all that information adds tremendously to the cost of the lawsuit. For this reason, ensuring that your organization has an appropriate record retention and deletion schedule is a critical risk management tool.

Tax Form 990, Part VI, Section B, Line 14, asks whether the organization has a written document retention and destruction policy. "A document retention and destruction policy identifies the record retention responsibilities of staff, volunteers, board members, and outsiders...."

KEY TAKEAWAYS

- You have a responsibility to act on information you have.

- Don't ask for information you don't need or can't reasonably process.

- Get permission to use personal information as intended.

- Protect personal data you gather, and don't keep it longer than necessary.

Implementation Tip 4: Review the applications your organization routinely uses to collect information from staff, customers, or stakeholders. Look at each question and ask *1) is the information requested really necessary?* and *2) what happens once you get it?* See if there is any detail you may be collecting that you may not really need.

Guiding Principle 5.

Once you act, you have to act reasonably.

This basic legal principle is the underpinning of most negligence claims. In many situations, we are not obligated to act, but once we do (for example, by offering a service or product), the law imposes a duty to act like reasonable and prudent people.

Good Samaritan laws provide some protection for volunteers who help strangers in an emergency.

> *"Simply put, Good Samaritan laws are there to protect people who selflessly jump in to help—without the expectation of a reward or accolades. They generally do not apply to paid medical or emergency rescue staff, as these people are getting paid for their services—not, from a legal standpoint at least, acting only out of the goodness of their hearts."*

https://www.cprcertified.com/blog/whats-in-those-good-samaritan-laws-exactly

Generally, people aren't legally required to stop and provide assistance to someone in distress (though they may be expected by law to call for help). However, if a person does stop, that person is expected to act reasonably.

For example, if an injured person is conscious, many states in the United States require the volunteer to ask the injured person for permission to help. (If the person is unconscious there is an implied consent to help.)

Laws vary by state. Some states may provide Good Samaritans with some immunity for their actions, but if the Good Samaritan is negligent in providing care and thereby worsens the injured person's condition, he or she may still be subject to a negligence claim.

Since even a stranger who stops to help someone in an emergency has a duty to act reasonably, it makes sense that a person whose job it is to provide services to support your organization is also expected to act reasonably.

If, for example, you run a summer camp for children with disabilities, you obviously have a duty to act reasonably in

> *Since responsibility begins when you decide to act, ask first if your organization should offer every service associated with your programs or if some might better be shifted to others.*

managing the risks associated with the camp, but you might not be required to do other things, such as provide transportation to and from the camp.

However, if you decide to offer transportation, you have an obligation to properly screen the company providing transportation and take steps to ensure any risks associated with the trip to and from the camp are managed appropriately.

When chartering a bus for a trip, for example, you have a duty to manage the risks associated with selecting the company. There are sites on the internet that allow you to look up the qualifications of chartered bus companies to help you make an informed selection. Other risks and responsibilities associated with transportation (such as getting insurance for the vehicles) can be shifted to the service provider.

"*Reasonable* in this context means exercising the care toward others that a reasonable or prudent person would under the circumstances."

You may also want to eliminate certain activities to avoid responsibility for them. If you serve alcohol at an event, for example, you may have a duty to manage the risk of someone leaving the event and driving while impaired. That's because the act of serving alcohol brings with it a duty to act reasonably in doing so.

- Negligence claims are grounded in the idea that once you act, you have a duty to act reasonably.

- Your organization should consider whether it *should* be providing all the services it does or might better shift some of those services to others.

- You should consider carefully the risks associated with products or services you provide that are not necessary for your mission or operations.

Implementation Tip 5: List the major activities or services your organization provides. Focus on describing *1) What is it that you do?* and *2) How do you deliver it?* Bring in your resident risk analysts (and more donuts). Ask them what they think it means to act reasonably or prudently in managing every circumstance on the list. Are there any circumstances that present too high a bar for your organization to meet consistently, or that perhaps should be managed differently?

Guiding Principle 6.

Treat people the same, unless there's a good reason to treat them differently.

Initially, this might sound like a legal theory grounded in discrimination laws, but in this case the basic principle is that everyone is entitled to the same level of risk management care.

People have a right to expect to receive the same level of protection, forethought, skills, and resources as any other

> *If someone is being treated differently, there should be a legitimate reason. Disclosing the reason may be prudent risk and expectation management.*

person in similar circumstances in your organization. Even if you have different funding, different locations, or different histories for certain volunteer programs within your organization, for example, know that these alone do not justify treating volunteers or customers differently when it comes to risk management protection.

Many mission-driven organizations rely on governmental or foundation support to carry out their activities. If funding is cut, certain programs may have to be cut. Sometimes, that may mean one group of volunteers continues to receive training while a similar group, possibly in a different location, can no longer continue training.

In this case, the risk you must manage remains the same; only the funding source has changed. If a claim is then filed based on a volunteer being inadequately trained, this could create a real loss for the organization.

However, there may be good reasons to treat people differently. In some cases, risks differ. You may have entirely different screening practices for different types of volunteers, and this makes perfect sense. Volunteers working with children need different screening than volunteers who drive meals to people's homes.

It may not be possible to offer similar treatment, even when that is your intention. Student exchange organizations that operate internationally face this challenge routinely, as visa requirements in each host country may impose different obligations.

The US J-1 visa requires that host families undergo a criminal background check in the vetting process. Unfortunately, criminal background checks are not possible in some countries. That leaves these organizations with no choice but to treat US-hosted students and students they send overseas differently. But in this case, there is a legitimate reason for doing so.

That does not absolve the organization from properly screening potential host families, but it does mean they can't screen every host family around the world in exactly the same way. They should consider letting potential travelers know how screening is handled, or about the background check limitation they face in some places.

> *Guiding Principle 6 is a reminder that it is important to treat similarly situated people the same way when possible, offering them the same level of risk management protection and care.*

At the same time, we are often forced to treat people differently for external reasons that are perfectly reasonable. However, to manage expectations, your organization needs to explain those differences.

If the differences can be managed in a way that provides comparable risk management protection to everyone, your organization stands a good chance of prevailing if a claim is filed. It stands an equally good chance of managing expectations if differences are addressed up front.

KEY TAKEAWAYS

- People expect and have a right receive the same level of risk management care as others in a similar situation.

- Different types of risk management approaches are fine if the risks or circumstances are different.

- Your organization should work to provide everyone with similar levels of protection, forethought, and risk management attention, even if it is not possible to manage risks in the same way in every case.

Implementation Tip 6: Consider the risks and risk management methods from the perspective of each of your stakeholders. Start with the premise that your approach should be applied consistently to all your stakeholders. Whenever you identify risks or methods unique to one group, ask 1) are the risks different, and 2) are the methods different. If the risks are different, it's reasonable to apply different risk management methods. If the methods are different but the risks are the same, stop and ask why. This is where you need to ensure that your organization is not letting one group down by failing to deliver risk management protections that are at least comparable to similarly situated people.

The mantra should be: *Provide similar levels of protection from similar risks by deploying comparable risk management methods wherever possible.*

Guiding Principle 7.

You can be held responsible for third parties if you have sufficient control over them.

It is a surprise, and an unpleasant one at times, for organizations to discover that they are legally responsible for the actions of people or groups that may not even be on their radar.

To understand this Guiding Principle, it's important to determine who your organization's stakeholders are, and then to assess whether you could be held legally responsible for their actions.

> *Companies can be responsible for employees and others who are acting on their behalf. This is often referred to as **vicarious** or **secondary liability.***

Nonprofits typically work closely with board members, trustees, donors, families, and community members, all of whom can be stakeholders.

Business stakeholders can include peer organizations, industry groups, suppliers and business strategic partners. Media can often be considered a stakeholder, too.

Not-for-profits and mission-driven organizations often rely on a wide variety of people and organizations to deliver their goods and services. Paid staff, volunteers, collaborative partners like schools or nongovernmental organizations, governmental agencies, third-party service providers such as transportation companies, consultants, and independent contractors may all be part of the mix. The distinctions among these groups can be blurry. It is extremely important to know and assess all your stakeholders carefully to avoid surprises.

Who Are Your Stakeholders?

On one end of the spectrum are employees—your paid staff. Organizations are responsible for their employees while they are doing their jobs and sometimes even for their activities outside the office, such as while on a business trip. This is based on the legal concept of vicarious liability and is a form of agency, based on an implied or actual "authority" to act on your organization's behalf.

In the United States, volunteers covered by the Volunteer Protection Act are people who provide services to charitable or not-for-profit organizations without significant compensation. Generally, the entities must be not-for-profit (or governmental), and the activity must be typically associated with volunteer work, be less than full time, and not displace regular workers.

Under the act, volunteers for a qualified not-for-profit generally will not be personally liable for harm caused if:

> *Unfortunately, whether your volunteers are paid or not is largely irrelevant to your organization's responsibility for them.*

1. They acted within the scope of their responsibilities.

2. They were properly licensed or certified (if required).

3. The harm was not caused by negligence or willful or reckless misconduct.

4. The harm was not caused by volunteers operating a motor vehicle, vessel, aircraft, or other vehicle for which the owner or operator is required to possess an operator's license or maintain insurance.

An organization can have a number of strategic business partners. These can include:

Independent contractors and third-party service providers—outside individuals or companies that provide services to you or your customers or other stakeholders for a fee.

> *An **agent** is someone authorized to act on your behalf. Agents can create the same type of secondary liability that an employer has for employees.*

Collaborative partners—organizations you work with to deliver services or products to your customers, such as other not-for-profits, schools, and governmental agencies.

Your organization can be legally vicariously responsible for any of these organizations or individuals under the legal theory of *agency*. Which of these parties are agents of your organization?

Unfortunately, it isn't always easy to determine. One thing is certain, assuming someone is not your agent but is acting independently for you does not remove your responsibility or the legal implications that arise with agency.

Employers should not be legally responsible for independent contractors, but it is often unclear whether someone is sufficiently independent for an employer to avoid responsibility.

The same is true for volunteers, consultants, and collaborative partners. Moreover, if the activity is inherently dangerous, hiring an independent contractor may not protect you from the responsibility of managing the risks involved.

One key is the *degree of control* you have over the person or group, regardless of whether you exercise that control. Whether the authority is actual (given by you), implied (needed to carry out the functions of the task), or apparent (through words or actions of the organization), if an organization has sufficient control, it can be found responsible for the agent's actions.

Let's say your organization operates weekend trips for city children to visit farms. You arrange for transportation to take the children to and from the farms and you train the farmers in what to do during the children's visit. The trip includes an overnight stay at nearby inns and an opportunity to milk cows, plant and harvest vegetables, and even cook healthy organic meals. Your organization includes the farmers in its liability insurance as additional insureds, so they would be protected from liability if an accident were to occur.

> *"Additional insured" usually refers to a person or entity added to coverage under an insurance policy by an endorsement, sometimes for a specific purpose or time period.*

If a child was injured by a runaway horse, or had a severe allergic reaction to a bee sting from the bee farm, could your organization be held responsible?

The answer is yes. But let's assume that your training program was very good, and you screened the farmers appropriately in all cases. In short, your organization was not negligent in any way.

Let's further assume that there was some negligence on the part of the farmer in each case. Perhaps the farmer failed to keep the horses properly fenced in, or failed to provide adequate protection for the children when gathering honey.

The question would then be whether the farmer was your agent. If so, his or her negligence can be imputed to your organization. The answer to the question often revolves around whether you exercise sufficient control over his or her actions.

> *In many cases, the simple fact that you provided training and insurance would be sufficient to find that a person or group is your agent.*

Laws vary in each state and around the world, so there are no easy answers to determining who can be considered your agent. However, the first step is to evaluate the stakeholders involved in your organization, including volunteers, external consultants, contractors, and collaborative partners, to determine whether they might be agents for whom you may be responsible.

When you provide services through third parties acting independently, clearly state that in your contracts with customers. Make clear in your materials and activities that these providers are acting independently and not under your direct supervision or control. Put the responsibility for being fully trained and insured on them.

Take note that, in many states, two key parts of a relationship can flag responsibility under agency: 1) providing liability insurance coverage, and 2) providing training.

Carefully review each group of stakeholders and the level of control you have over them to ensure that your risk management program encompasses all the people and organizations that might create liability and pose a risk for your organization. Organizations that ignore this Guiding Principle when identifying organizational risk can leave themselves very vulnerable.

KEY TAKEAWAYS

- Identify people your organization can be responsible for whom you may not even be thinking about (e.g., third parties), if you have sufficient control over their activities.

- Evaluate the role and level of control you have for all your stakeholders.

- Manage the risks associated with each group by either exercising proper oversight and control or making clear in your materials and activities that they are independent contractors and you are NOT responsible for them.

Implementation Tip 7: Who could be considered to be your agent? Investigate who in your organization, other than staff— such as independent contractors, volunteers, or collaborative partners—might *receive training* or *insurance coverage* from you.

Guiding Principle 8.

Meeting expectations avoids claims—therefore it's a key element of managing risks.

Quality Risk Management looks beyond the classic threat of litigation to manage a wider range of risks, including losses arising from unrealistic expectations and customer dissatisfaction.

> *Whose expectations matter? Those of all your stakeholders.*

As most of the Guiding Principles show, allegations of negligence are a primary source of litigation and blame for not-for-profit and mission-driven organizations. We have shown you key ways to frame and understand these allegations.

But can your organization encounter claims and allegations even if you haven't been negligent? Yes! Can these occur even if you believe you've identified risks, acted on them, disclosed them and managed them all adequately—even when you've obtained informed consents, dealt with the issues of agency, and made the effort to treat people the same way? Of course they can.

What if you're not to blame for a bad situation? Could someone still hold you responsible for what she or he thinks is a bad outcome? These days, it's easy for anyone to use the internet to vent, accuse, or spread an opinion worldwide, at no personal investment or cost. The potential damage to your reputation is immense. This is a modern and rapidly expanding organizational risk.

Unfortunately, doing everything right to avoid negligence does not ensure complete protection. Wrongly sued or publicly blamed, you can still face losses even if you are eventually proven correct. That might require legal expense, which can be another form of loss for you. Annoying complaints can cause a drip-drip deterioration in morale, loss of company time, and even a loss of customers or donors.

Problems like this can take a toll on credibility, reputation, funding, and resources, such as customers or volunteers. Those are intangible losses, the kinds that aren't protected by insurance.

This is why we view management of intangible risk as important to your organization as management of true negligence, and why it's a key component in Quality Risk Management.

What kind of risk are we talking about? What would cause someone to make an allegation or complaint about something that you believe is undeserved? The best way to evaluate this is by looking at it as an *expectation that is not being met.*

Negligence lays out a legal standard for conduct that is widely acknowledged. But if you are meeting that standard and still getting complaints, that means another kind of standard is in play, even if it's not as recognizable. That other standard arises as an expectation, and it can cause loss if it's not met.

Here's an example: Managers of a highly regarded summer camp are stunned when angry parents threaten to sue over emergency medical care provided to their camper after a sudden illness.

The organization staff thought they did exactly the right and reasonable things to save the camper's life in pursuing immediate emergency medical care. They are relieved and happy that she is safely in recovery.

But the camper's parents believe they should have been more fully involved in her care decisions. They think they could have been contacted as soon as the emergency occurred. They say that they would have advocated a different path for medical care. They accuse the camp of incompetent management and of endangering their child.

"Are they out of their minds?" the camp managers wonder. "There's no way we could have consulted them in the timeframe we had. They weren't here. They don't know what we were dealing with! We're lucky things turned out as well as they did. We deserve thanks, not complaints." They're horrified to see reports of their alleged mismanagement on social media.

Two sets of expectations clash here. One is the organization's, expecting to be acknowledged for having acted with reasonable care, for having done the right thing.

When we consult with organizations, we often poll them about examples of mismatched expectations.

But the parents have their own expectations. Even when they signed an authorization for the organization to act in a medical emergency, they still expected that care would be provided in a certain way and don't understand why they could not have been called sooner. They believe that had they been contacted, their intervention early on could have changed the course of medical treatment. This may be unreasonable, but it was still their expectation.

In consulting with organizations, we ask whom they'd call first in a medical emergency. Usually it's a call for an ambulance, which is smart. But when we ask them what parents would expect them to do first, they'll often shift uncomfortably, saying that parents might indeed expect to be contacted first. They're often aware of conflicting expectations. Organizations will typically satisfy both when they can, but they won't fulfill both when one conflicts with common-sense necessary care, in their judgment. That's reasonable, but it doesn't always prevent complaints.

This is an example of an expectation that needs to be understood and addressed, because it can derail what would otherwise be a positive outcome, based on sound risk management.

How can this type of risk be managed? The first step is to determine who your stakeholders are. Who are the people or entities that may have expectations about your services or products from the perspective of "acting reasonably under the circumstances?" Your analysis should include what their expectations might be—whether you think these expectations are reasonable or not.

"I'm right there in the room, and no one even acknowledges me."

When the organization is aware that parents have an emergency contact expectation, even one that may not line up with what it can deliver, the organization should address that head-on. The organization can explain more fully what parents should expect in its management of a medical emergency.

In this case, the explanation could be in the wording of the waiver or permission forms, or in the agreements it makes or discussions it has with parents before the camping session begins. If parents do not agree, they have the option to say so, or to pull their child from the camp before something happens.

This is an example of the way setting policies helps set expectations. In our experience, unmet expectations get too little attention in traditional risk management. By addressing them up front in your overall approach to risk management—by combining quality with risk management—you can help protect your organization's reputation and brand using known risk management methods.

Generally, there are three things you can do when dealing with an expectation like the one in this example.

> **1. Meet the expectation.** To do this, determine that parents should be called within the expected timeframe, and train your people to do that.

> **2. Change the expectation.** If you can't call parents that quickly, but you could call them within a longer timeframe, inform parents, staff, volunteers, and all involved in advance of the timeframe you would use to notify.

3. Don't meet the expectation. If you can't set a timeframe, you need to let parents know up front that you can't guarantee when you will be able to reach them, or that you will be able to reach them at all, although you can assure them that you will make your best efforts to do so.

Some organizations find it's helpful to explain the effort that went into creating the policy in order to unpack the expectations around it.

> *It pays to manage expectations, because satisfied people don't sue or complain.*

When you tell people what they can expect from you and why, and then you follow through, people are often satisfied, even if the outcome is not what they wanted.

In fact, many people experience tragedy and loss without suing. If customers feel that your organization did all they expected it to do, then even when there's a loss, you have gone a long way to effectively managing the risk of a complaint or lawsuit.

KEY TAKEAWAYS

- Losses can arise not only from negligence claims but also from unmet expectations.

- Managing expectations, realistic or not, is a critical element of Quality Risk Management.

- Complaints coming from unmet expectations can cause serious damage to an organization in a short time, and most of the potential harm can't be insured.

- Managing expectations requires identifying and addressing your stakeholders' expectations in advance.

- Expectations can be managed by meeting them, changing them, or making clear in advance that you cannot meet them.

- People who are satisfied with your product or service won't sue, and rarely complain.

Implementation Tip 8: Know who your stakeholders are. Going from specific to general, consider who within the organization *has a stake in how the organization performs*. This includes board members, volunteers, and participants. Expand to entities outside the organization, such as vendors or funders. Finally, consider entities that are not directly connected to your organization but would weigh in regardless, such as local leaders, trade associations, or government agencies.

Guiding Principle 9.

Standards help manage expectations, but having one you don't follow is worse than not having one.

People evaluate their experiences based on their expectations. Meeting your customers' expectations is the best way to ensure their satisfaction with your products and services.

But expectations have many different sources: laws, past experience, the experiences that others have—even cultural and social norms can set expectations. So understanding your customers' and other stakeholders' expectations is a critical part of managing expectations.

> *Standards help eliminate unrealistic expectations and help organizations maintain consistency. They establish the baseline of what stakeholders can and can't expect of you.*

Standards are bases of comparison that help manage expectations. An external authority or your organization can produce a standard. Either way, it must be available for everyone to see and use to assess how an organization is performing.

As a society we think positively of people and organizations that have high standards, and we consider such standards a sign of good management.

"We'll keep your application on file and if we ever lower our standards, we'll give you a call."

Using standards is very helpful for organizations in risk management, but it has to be a very thoughtful practice, because it carries its own risks.

Consider bullying in schools. All 50 U.S. states have enacted laws that require public schools to implement policies and procedures that prevent or stop bullying. This is an example of an external legal standard with which schools must comply.

Schools have been eager to deal effectively with this problem, and parents and families fully expect this. As a result, many schools implemented a zero-tolerance standard for dealing with bullying as a means of declaring their commitment. This became an internally created standard for many schools.

Policies and implementation procedures backed up the standard. For example, one of the policies often associated with the standard is that bringing a weapon to school constitutes bullying.

However, zero-tolerance standards required that predetermined consequences, such as suspension or expulsion, had to apply in every case, regardless of circumstances. One school had a situation it thought qualified as a special circumstance. A child inadvertently brought a plastic knife in his lunch box to cut an apple. However, the school, because of its zero-tolerance standard, was unable to take this into consideration and had to expel the child.

A zero-tolerance standard is an example of how oppressive a standard can be and how it can lead to unintended consequences. Zero-tolerance shows its

> *Standards are not goals or guidelines; they are promises you make to the public.*

greatest limitation right in its name. Many schools have replaced the zero-tolerance standard not because they want to be more tolerant of bullying, but because they want to be able to offer more nuanced, appropriate responses for each case.

In the case of anti-bullying standards, if zero-tolerance can't be reliably applied in every case, it needs to be adjusted. A different standard might be that the school promises to address each case involving bullying as fully and effectively as it can. Then the school can create a toolkit of policies and procedures that support this, setting up consistent compliance throughout the organization.

The difference between a policy or a procedure and a standard is that once you have published a standard, you must meet it 100% of the time. Internal procedures and guidelines don't set expectations the way published standards do.

Once you have made a public promise in the form of a standard, you must uphold it. Any lapse opens an easy door to liability and complaints, because you have already demonstrated its importance by creating and publishing it. There is little protection for you when someone with a claim or complaint can point right to what you said you would uphold, but did not. Moreover, it's easy to see that failing to meet published standards increases the likelihood of complaints.

> *When there are no clear standards, people often apply their own expectations, realistic or not.*

You might be asking, "If internally created standards are so demanding, why would you want to set them?" The answer is if you have no standards, you create uncertainty and the potential that what you do will not match peoples' expectations.

When you create and implement your own standards, you can also create the policies and procedures that support them, upholding your

> *Support what you say you'll do with appropriate policies, procedures, training, and resources.*

principles and protecting your organization.

Before developing any standard, consider whether it really is a promise that you want to and can keep. Before implementing each standard, ask yourself, "Are we going to be able to make sure we uphold this every time, without fail?" If that's not possible, adjust the standard. If circumstances like funding, personnel, or training limitations make it difficult to consistently meet the standard, rethink it.

What if the organization finds that it can't uphold even an adjusted standard? Then it is probably best not to have it. Instead, let stakeholders know of your best efforts, but be upfront in stating that their expectations may not always be met. Put them in the position to decide to work with you under the terms you offer, even if those terms aren't exactly what they may have desired.

This is why internally created standards are such helpful risk management tools for managing expectations on your terms. When you can't meet expectations, creating standards you can meet clarifies what can actually be expected of you. Be careful not to over-promise, as failing to meet a published standard is an invitation to litigation and unmet expectations.

KEY TAKEAWAYS

- Organizations are expected to meet standards that apply to them. Failing to do so exposes them to litigation and complaints.

- Standards can be set externally or internally.

- Internally created standards help manage expectations, even unrealistic ones, and support consistency in providing services.

- If your organization has established standards, they should be supported by policies and procedures, because it's critical these standards are met 100% of the time.

Implementation Tip 9: Distinguish between internal standards and the procedures and policies that are in play in your organization. Which are upheld 100% of the time? If a standard isn't always upheld, it should not be a standard. If you are consistently getting complaints about something, consider establishing a standard that's appropriate to manage those expectations.

Guiding Principle 10.

You have a duty to be aware of and comply with standards that apply to you.

The laws, regulations, guidelines, and standards that apply to any business are changing quite rapidly. One scandal, such as a highly publicized food poisoning case arising from a restaurant, a volunteer kitchen, or a big fundraising event can result in new requirements for food management, even though the mechanisms may not yet be in place for everyone to carry them out effectively.

A single event can generate hearings and new laws and regulations with far-reaching implications for other organizations.

September 11th dramatically altered the way any international organization operates. For example, ever-tighter visa restrictions have challenged these organizations (and businesses of all kinds), making it more difficult for students to travel abroad or workers to come to the United States.

Unfortunately, as the adage goes, "ignorance of the law is no excuse." The same can be said of standards.

> *In a sense, standards are the minimum level of service delivery or product quality that applies to your operations.*

Organizations must constantly monitor governmental and industry-related entities that apply to their operations to stay current with applicable laws and standards. For example, the National Fire Protective Association sets standards for fire departments. And monitoring is only the beginning, for they must comply with these standards as well.

When considering this Guiding Principle, look at standards in the broadest sense to include not only internally created or industry-wide quality standards, but also all the general laws, rules, and regulations that apply to your organization.

The Centers for Disease Control, for example, have determined that motor vehicle crashes are the leading cause of death for children in the United States, and motor vehicle injuries are their greatest public health problem.

Based on risk information like this, the National Highway Transportation Safety Administration, a U.S. government agency, maintains extensive regulatory standards for school buses, requiring a higher level of safety than regular buses. These are examples of external standards that apply to schools.

Local school districts or municipalities that make their own rules about how students must use the buses in their district are creating internal standards. Even though the school district or town itself created them, schools are still expected to follow them 100% of the time.

> *Organizations carrying out activities with little current regulation should seriously consider developing their own standards or collaborating with other organizations in their field to develop common standards.*

Some organizations operate in heavily regulated areas, such as construction or health care. Others may be less regulated. But all not-for-profits or mission-driven organizations are subject to significant state and federal rules relating to taxes, governance, and fundraising. Every organization has some external standards that govern its behavior.

Setting your own internal standards can help you manage expectations. However, as discussed in the previous Guiding Principle, you need to use great care in developing standards to avoid raising expectations beyond what you can consistently deliver.

Don't wait for the public, the courts or the legislature to tell you how to operate. When organizations create their own standards, they have the opportunity to shape them in a way that allows them to build on their strengths, which can make compliance much easier.

This also enables them to manage stakeholders' expectations more effectively, because organizations tend to know their stakeholders much better than the lawmakers or other parties who are more removed from day-to-day programs and activities.

When not-for-profits do an excellent job of self-regulating their activities with appropriate standards and compliance programs, they can avoid over-regulation.

But when they fail to set expectations at the right level with appropriate industry standards, this can lead to unrealistic expectations and reputation-damaging stories playing out on the internet. These can make it difficult to respond

> *If others think that you or your industry are not setting sufficiently high standards, legislators, courts, and even the general public will tend to set them for you, either through the law or through public opinion.*

effectively and to continue to provide programs with the limited budgets so many mission-driven organizations face.

Essentially, this Guiding Principle is about awareness of when compliance is expected and how to make it work for your protection, as well as for the protection of your stakeholders.

Compliance can only occur successfully when the organization has put the mechanisms and systems in place that allow it to monitor applicable laws, regulations, and standards and to successfully meet the burdens of the applicable laws and standards.

When legislators react to tragedy, their response can swiftly lead to new laws and regulations, even with insufficient input from affected businesses, especially not-for-profits. The resulting burdens created by new standards can be quite heavy.

Most organizations understand they must comply with the law, but those that operate internationally often face conflicting and unclear obligations. Take privacy, for example.

In the United States, courts have tended to set a low bar for the level of privacy we are entitled to and, though this is changing, people in the U.S. tend to have a lower expectation of privacy. The European Union has developed much more demanding obligations for organizations that process data of EU citizens, where expectations of privacy are significantly higher.

If you operate internationally, are you clear about what data processing and privacy laws apply to your operations? Moreover, can you clarify expectations so that you not only meet legal requirements but also ensure that your customers don't expect more than you can deliver?

Because the standards that apply to your organization will continue to evolve, it is critical that your compliance program include regular monitoring of changes to standards that can affect not only your operations, but also the effectiveness of your compliance program. You should even scrutinize your internally created standards periodically to ensure they continue to reflect what your organization can do and what others expect of your organization.

KEY TAKEAWAYS

- Organizations must comply with ALL the standards that apply to them, including laws and regulations, as well as industry-wide and internally created standards.

- If you operate in a less-regulated industry, creating your own standards is an extremely valuable risk management tool, as it manages expectations, shows prudent business practices, and helps align your internal training and compliance programs with your operations.

- Your risk management program should include regular monitoring of all applicable standards and periodic review of your own standards to ensure alignment and compliance.

Implementation Tip 10: In addition to the external standards that apply to you, identify three *internal standards* that help stakeholders understand and measure your performance. How could they help you manage expectations?

Guiding Principle 11.

A compassionate response is critical—especially when loss is significant.

Historically, organizations were advised to say "no comment" after a loss happened or a crisis occurred. They were told to refer questions to others and stand back from an emerging problem to reduce their liability. That often did not feel right and it made those affected more upset.

When accidents or injuries happen, we care deeply, and it seems odd and disconnected when we don't express that in an appropriate way.

> *There is a big difference between saying, "we care about what happened," and "we are at fault." It is possible to be compassionate without increasing liability.*

Experience has shown us that a compassionate response to a loss is not only what you think you should provide, but it's also good risk management. After all, in most cases people expect a compassionate response.

Train your staff and volunteers not to discuss liability, make promises, or speculate when they talk about a loss or are dealing with a crisis. But encourage them to be personal and show that they care.

Gather facts and offer support at the highest levels of your organization. Anticipate family needs, assist with logistics, listen, acknowledge, stay in regular touch, and let all those involved know they are important and that resolution of the situation is your top priority.

As we have discussed, liability for many not-for-profit and mission-based organizations often revolves around allegations of negligence—the failure to meet reasonable expectations. Whether there is negligence is rarely clear at the outset. You might be certain that your organization bears no fault, but being at the center of an allegation already creates the potential for damage.

A swift and thoughtful response to a situation where negligence is a concern is the right thing to do. Not only does it focus your energy on helping those most affected, it can show your organization in a favorable light to outsiders who will naturally empathize with anyone suffering or experiencing a bad outcome.

When a loss first occurs, consider the following:

- Determine if any medical or emergency attention is needed.

- Try to put a stop to whatever caused the loss until it can be more fully reviewed.

- Get anyone or anything at risk out of harm's way. Implement your crisis management plan, especially your crisis communications plan.

- Try to find out the facts behind what happened. Investigate if needed.

- Inform the stakeholders involved in the loss and try to respond to them right away, without delay.

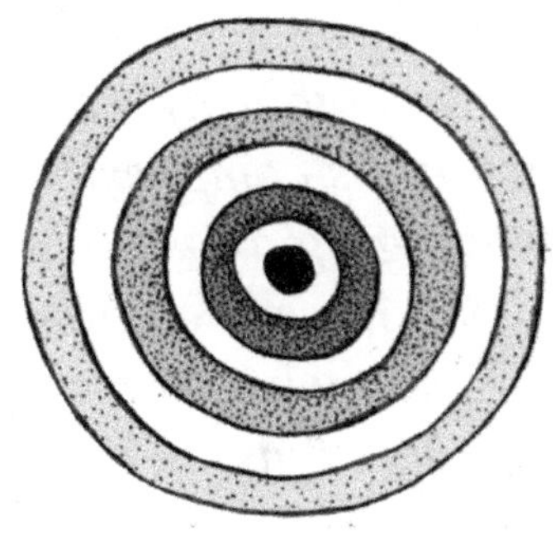

Consider the circumstance of the loss like a bull's eye. At the center are the parties directly involved. Radiating out from that are parties experiencing the loss indirectly. They all need support and attention.

An example is an accusation of molestation against an organization's director. Of course the claimant deserves your primary attention. But also consider participants, staff, families, or volunteers who may be shocked and wondering, or customers who may hear about the matter on social media.

> *A compassionate response can forestall a complaint or keep a complaint from turning into a lawsuit.*

All of these need care. Reach out to them quickly with the factual information you have and show concern by being attentive to their needs. Be prepared for others to come forward with similar complaints and consider what kind of investigation is appropriate.

One of the surprising things we have found about complaints and even lawsuits is that people don't necessarily lodge them because terrible things have happened. They will often complain or sue because they are angry or upset at the way they think they were treated, or the poor way they believe a matter was handled.

They want to be heard and to be treated with respect and empathy. They want to feel supported after having had a bad experience, even while presenting themselves as adversarial or confrontational.

It can be difficult, because in times of high stress the messenger often does seem to take

> *It is possible for an organization's reputation to grow as a result of its compassion in managing a loss. You may not have been able to prevent what happened, but you can contribute greatly to what happens afterwards.*

the brunt, even if the person delivering the message and the organization are not at fault. This can shift over time, however, as facts come out, and those affected receive and process the support and compassion expressed.

The remarkable thing about the compassionate response is that it can be at its most powerful in the direst of situations, such as the death or grave injury of a participant.

We have seen this Guiding Principle help bridge relationships that resulted in lasting mutual respect rather than litigation. We've seen a grieving family help fund a scholarship program in honor of their late child with the organization that they initially approached with despair and rage about her death. Both parties were able to reveal to the other how sad they were, how much was lost, how they could move forward and honor this young person.

Much of risk management involves either preventing or reducing the likelihood of a loss. Loss response is often under-appreciated as a risk management tool, as people tend to view a loss as a risk management failure. When a loss has occurred, they may think the course of the loss is fixed and its outcome predetermined. They throw in the towel and focus on self-protection.

In fact, a loss can always happen, even when risk of loss is largely successfully prevented or mitigated. When it does occur, think about what you would hope to hear from the organization involved if the loss were to happen to you. Be generous in offering genuine care and assistance. Try to meet and exceed that human expectation, and let the legal, insurance, and financial discussions happen in their appropriate ways.

KEY TAKEAWAYS

- Managing losses once they occur is just as important as trying to prevent losses from occurring.

- Losses that affect people personally deserve an empathetic and compassionate response.

- Responding compassionately need not increase liability if handled properly.

- Having a crisis management plan, including crisis communications, and having people prepared to respond and provide support is critical to managing crises.

Implementation Tip 11: Bring in your insurance broker or another insurance professional. Set up a training session for personnel involved in crisis management, customer care, and outreach or support. Discuss the differences between liability, responsibility, and insurance. Help them become comfortable in understanding the difference between admitting fault and offering support. Offer phrasing or terminology they can use so that they can say what they mean at times of loss, with compassion and confidence. Consider also what additional support might be expected, such as counseling after a tragedy, or credit monitoring after a data breach.

4

Quality Management and Risk Management

As you have seen throughout the Guiding Principles, Quality Risk Management blends quality management and risk management techniques.

Quality management provides the tools for understanding and managing expectations. Risk management provides the tools for dealing with liability. Together they make up Quality Risk Management— an approach that manages potential losses that can arise from legal liability (like negligence) as well as losses that arise from unmet expectations.

Combining quality management and risk management results in a more holistic and effective risk management program.

The major difference between classic quality management and classic risk management is the way they are used. Quality management is typically about making improvements, while risk management is seen as addressing responsibility. One feels voluntary; the other seems mandated.

Both disciplines help an organization prevent bad outcomes. Both disciplines are concerned with meeting stakeholder expectations, and both deal with managing the difficulties when those aren't met. When these issues arise, quality management efforts reduce risk because satisfied customers are less likely to complain and sue.

Because managing both processes is quite similar, we have found they can be integrated into the same program using the Quality Risk Management approach. An organization using Quality Risk Management can gain the benefit of both disciplines while producing better outcomes and protecting its reputation.

Another benefit of combining the disciplines is that quality management is a great motivator. People like to be associated with delivering high quality and with organizations that have good reputations.

Quality Risk Management can also be a valuable tool for getting the financial and human resource support needed in organizations to meet risk management goals.

5

Using the Guiding Principles for Better Outcomes

Bad outcomes often come from people's expectations about the way a loss occurred, not necessarily from the loss itself. It's possible for an organization to have performed well and for others involved in the loss to say, "This was an awful thing that happened, but we understand what you did. We appreciate the support you provided."

> *It's possible for a loss to occur and for many positive things to come out of the experience. Your organization can emerge stronger than it was before.*

Unless Quality Risk Management is in place, however, that's not usually what happens.

The definition of negligence we are using is "failing to act reasonably under all circumstances." The question that usually arises in evaluating responsibility for a loss is what actions can be considered reasonable. That issue is further complicated by people's expectations, realistic or not.

It's very easy for an outcome to become adverse when everyone's expectations differ. An organization may feel it is doing the right thing, while its customers are expecting something totally different. The mismatch is what leads to losses.

Why are not-for-profits and mission-driven organizations particularly subject to high expectations? Primarily, it is because they often serve vulnerable populations, such as children, the elderly, or the infirm, and this client base demands a higher standard of care than is applicable to many business ventures.

For example, a university carries a very high standard of care for dormitory security, despite the challenges of keeping buildings secure while students expect to be able to move freely in and among them.

What sets this higher standard of care? Standards themselves, when they are in effect; otherwise it is the expectations of those involved. Being unaware of these expectations is a leading cause of complaints, and can lead to unexpected losses.

Example Revisited

Think back to the example cited in the eighth Guiding Principle: *Meeting expectations avoids claims; therefore, it's a key element of managing risks.*

This was the story of the parents who were angry at the organization when their child needed emergency care. They thought they were not informed quickly enough, even though, fortunately, their daughter recovered.

> *A fundamental underpinning of the Quality Risk Management method is that people complain or sue because their expectations are not met.*

The organization believed it did the right thing, both by the child and by the parents, and insisted that it simply was not possible during the emergency to reach the parents as quickly as the parents expected. That seemed reasonable from the organization's perspective, but the parents had different expectations.

The organization cited all the steps they had taken to obtain medical help.

They were tremendously relieved that the child was all right and shocked to receive the parents' complaint. It alleged that the organization's actions went on too long without their involvement, endangering the child's health. The parents expected the organization to perform with a speed the organization did not think was possible.

Although the decisions about the child's health care may not have changed at all had the parents been on the scene earlier, the matter became clouded by the parents' allegation.

Now the issue had to be evaluated to see whether, in fact, calling the parents earlier was a reasonable expectation—whether this could have been accomplished and whether that could have changed the situation.

The parents' complaint also appeared on social media, creating doubt about the organization's trustworthiness, which the organization found difficult to counteract without appearing to attack the family.

This is an example of a pretty bad outcome arising from stakeholders' expectations, when in fact the organization responded reasonably, and the situation itself ended up being not so terrible.

Take the thinking a little further: if the medical emergency had not turned out as well as it did, the organization would have badly needed much more clarity about the reasonableness of the expectations to survive a lawsuit. And the parents would have clearly blamed the organization for the outcome, even though the organization believed it had acted without fault.

Quality Risk Management can help prevent these potential losses by including managing expectations in your risk management program.

Using the Guiding Principles for Quality Risk Management

What could the organization have done to achieve a better outcome? You can see that this organization could have managed the issues encountered by following the Guiding Principles of Quality Risk Management.

GP 1. Identify the risks that could produce the need for emergency medical care without guaranteeing safety.

GP 2. Disclose the risks to the family.

GP 3. Get fully informed consent from the family.

GP 4. Obtain all necessary information about the child's health and act on that information.

GP 5. Figure out what it means to act reasonably, once a decision is made to seek medical care in emergencies.

GP 6. Ensure any actions taken to care for the child would be the same as for any other child, unless there is a legitimate reason to treat her differently.

GP 7. Understand the organization can be held responsible for the actions of any third parties who might act on its behalf as agents (if the organization has sufficient control over them).

GP 8. Anticipate the expectations of the family in a medical emergency.

GP 9. Let the family know how the organization would manage such a situation, and be able to demonstrate that it lives up to its standards consistently.

GP 10. Comply with any applicable external standards.

GP 11. Offer a compassionate response to let the family know the organization cares, and provide support without admitting fault or liability.

These simple principles support a broader approach to risk management, allowing your organization to address the range of losses that can occur, all the way from the traditional concepts of liability to the Wild West of unmet expectations. Using the Guiding Principles would have helped this organization better manage the situation and minimize losses and complaints.

6

Putting Quality Risk Management to Use

No Complaints, No Lawsuits is a first step toward understanding the Guiding Principles behind Quality Risk Management. It presents the big picture. It's beyond the scope of this book to go into great detail. However, we can wrap up with a review of what goes into Quality Risk Management as we combine its two components.

Managing Risk With Quality Risk Management

A risk is a chance of loss. We developed Quality Risk Management to deal more broadly with the chance of loss and to anticipate losses more readily than traditional risk management allows. This is especially true of uninsurable losses, like reputational damage, which depend on meeting customer expectations.

You've always known that an organization faces the risk of allegations of negligence arising from a bad outcome. Now you know that an allegation—as big as a lawsuit, as small as a complaint—can be fueled by unmet expectations as well as by legal fault. This requires expanding the traditional breadth of risk management by using Quality Risk Management.

> *Managing expectations is not the same as assuming liability for everything that happens, or of trying to control every outcome.*

Managing liability is not simply about managing actual fault. The situation often revolves around managing expectations, which can help prevent losses and limit bad outcomes.

The loss of intangibles, such as reputation, funders, morale, or participants, is also poorly addressed by traditional risk management methods. Insurance can't restore these kinds of assets, so organizations are particularly vulnerable to loss from unmet expectations. Managing the chance of loss of intangibles through Quality Risk Management is an important addition to classic risk management.

Managing expectations puts the organization in the position of better preparing for the full range of risks before they turn into losses. This is why both risk management and Quality Risk Management, as separate disciplines, operate with similar thinking—that we must first determine what risks and expectations are in play and then figure out what to do about them.

Risk Management Steps

The four well-known steps in classic risk management are:

1) Identify risk.

2) Assess its impact (frequency and severity).

3) Control or otherwise manage the risk.

4) Monitor the risk management program.

Crucial elements of quality management are to:

1) identify stakeholders

2) determine their expectations and where they
   originate

3) develop standards for the organization to use in
   creating policies and managing expectations

4) monitor policy success.

Risk assessment for Quality Risk Management is a composite of these systems. It involves both identifying classic liability risks and hazards and identifying stakeholders.

For example, an environmental conservancy deals with the risks of managing natural areas. Typically it would focus on marking areas of hazard, providing information and using signage to let people know what they should and should not do. It might put up a notice—*No Hunting*. Using Quality Risk Management, we'd also assess who the stakeholders are, from visitors to trespassers to neighbors to local government to funders. What are their assumptions about hunting? Do some people believe it is going to happen anyway, while others assume they will be safe from it?

This requires determining stakeholder expectations and where those expectations come from, such as local regulations, usual practices, and understanding the rules and other internal and external standards that may apply. Assessing how identified risks and expectations interact illuminates what we call *risk themes*. Risk themes show us how loss really happens.

The next step is to set risk management priorities, using classic risk control methods, such as reducing or transferring risk, in addition to building standards that address the expectations identified in the risk themes.

> *Assessing expectations in proper relationship to applicable standards— by meeting them, changing them, or determining the standard can't be met— is a very effective risk control method, and it's born from quality management.*

Efforts to manage loss by increasing quality can't involve making temporary upgrades that could be suspended at will. It's important to follow through and be consistent. Remember the tenth Guiding Principle—standards help manage expectations, but having a standard you don't follow is worse than not having one.

Fortunately, the marriage of risk and quality in Quality Risk Management provides a set of tools that classic risk management has been missing—a systematic means of determining how well the risk management plan is working to address the full range of losses that arise, from complaints all the way to lawsuits.

Quality Risk Management uses not just loss and hazard information records but stakeholder feedback in adjusting risk management as it matures and as the organization's risks shift. Knowing your stakeholders and understanding their expectations through continuous program monitoring ensures that your risk management can evolve brilliantly, even as your organization continues to grow.

www.ingramcontent.com/pod-product-compliance
Lightning Source LLC
Chambersburg PA
CBHW071447030726
47593CB00003B/931